VEGAN BARBECUE

ULTIMATE SMOKER COOKBOOK FOR REAL VEGANS, IRRESISTIBLE RECIPES FOR UNIQUE VEGAN BBQ

BY ADAM JONES

TABLE OF CONTENTS

INTRODUCTION

Smoking meat or making BBQ is not only a means of cooking but for some individuals and classy enthusiasts, this is a form of Art! Or dare I say a form of lifestyle! Enthusiasts all around the world have been experimenting and dissecting the secrets of perfectly smoked meat for decades now, and in our golden age, perhaps they have cracked it up completely! In our age, the technique of Barbecuing or Smoking meat has been perfected to such a level, that a BBQ Grill is pretty much an essential amenity found in all backyard or sea-beach parties!

This is the drinking fountain for the more hip and adventurous people, who

prefer to have a nice chat with their friends and families while smoking up a few batches of Burger Patty for them to enjoy. But here's the thing, while this art might seem as a very easy form of cooking which only requires you to flip meats over and over! Mastering it might be a little bit difficult if you don't know have the proper information with you. And that is exactly why I have written this chapter, where I will walk you through the very basic elements of Smoking, so that you may start off experimenting with the recipes in no time at all! Let's start with a very basic question, the answer to which should be known to all budding smokers and master pitters out there!

FIND MORE INFORMATION ABOUT VEGAN LIFESTYLE AND VEGAN BARBECUE AT THE END OF THE BOOK

CHAPTER 1 - VEGETABLES

SMOKED BELL PEPPER WITH VEGGIE FILLING

(TOTAL COOK TIME 1 HOUR 10 MINUTES)

INGREDIENTS FOR 10 SERVINGS

- Bell pepper (3-lbs., 1.361-kgs)

THE FILLING

- Diced eggplant – ½ cup

- Diced cucumber – ½ cup

- Diced yellow squash – ¼ cup

- Diced onion – ½ cup

- Minced garlic – 2 teaspoons

- Olive oil – 1 ½ tablespoons

- Dried thyme – ½ teaspoon

- Salt – ¼ teaspoon

- Black pepper – ½ teaspoon

THE HEAT

- Maple wood

METHOD

1. Prepare the smoker for indirect heat and set the temperature to 300°F (149°C). Wait until the smoker reaches the desired temperature.

2. Meanwhile, place diced eggplant, diced zucchini, diced yellow squash, and diced onion in a bowl.

3. Drizzle olive oil over the vegetables then season with minced garlic, dried thyme, salt, and black pepper. Mix well then set aside.

4. Cut the bell peppers into halves lengthwise then scoop out the seeds.

5. Fill the bell peppers with the vegetables mixture then place in the smoker.

6. Close the smoker and smoke the stuffed bell peppers for about an hour.

7. Once it is done, take the smoked stuffed bell peppers out of the smoker then arrange on a serving dish.

8. Serve and enjoy warm.

SMOKED EGGPLANT WITH SWEET LEMON TOPPING

(TOTAL COOK TIME 1 HOUR 10 MINUTES)

INGREDIENTS FOR 10 SERVINGS

- Eggplants (3-lbs., 1.361-kgs)

THE RUB

- Salt – 2 teaspoons
- Canola oil – 3 tablespoons

THE TOPPING

- Olive oil – ½ cup

- Minced shallots – 2 ½ teaspoons

- Lemon juice – 2 tablespoons

- Coconut sugar – 2 teaspoons

- Salt – ¼ teaspoon

- Minced parsley – 2 tablespoons

THE HEAT

- Maesquite wood

METHOD

1. Prepare the smoker for indirect heat and set the temperature to 225°F (107°C).

2. While waiting for the smoke, cut the eggplants into halves lengthwise then brush each part with canola oil.

3. Sprinkle salt over the eggplants and once the smoke is ready, arrange the eggplants on the rack inside the smoker.

4. Smoke the eggplants for an hour or until tender.

5. In the meantime, combine olive oil with lemon juice then mix well.

6. Add minced shallots, coconut sugar, salt, and minced garlic to the liquid mixture then stir until combined. Set aside.

7. Once the smoked eggplant is done, remove from the smoker and cut into thick slices.

8. Arrange the smoked eggplant slices on a serving dish then drizzle the spice mixture on top.

9. Serve and enjoy.

Smoked Portobello Mushroom Garlic

(total cook time 2 Hours 5 Minutes)

Ingredients for 10 servings

- Portobello mushroom (3-lbs., 1.361-kgs)

The Glaze

- Olive oil – ¼ cup
- Worcestershire sauce – ¼ cup

- Chopped garlic – 1 ½ tablespoons

- Hot sauce – 1 teaspoon

- Chopped tomatoes – ¼ cup

- Chopped onions – ¼ cup

THE HEAT

- Masquite wood

METHOD

1. Wash and rinse the Portobello mushroom under running water then pat them dry.

2. Prepare the smoker for indirect heat and set the temperature to 225°F (107°C). wait until the smoker is ready.

3. In the meantime, place chopped garlic, chopped onions, tomatoes, and hot sauce in a blender.

4. Pour olive oil and Worcestershire sauce into the blender then blend until smooth.

5. Once the smoke is ready, place the Portobello mushrooms on the rack inside the smoker.

6. Smoke the Portobello mushrooms for approximately 2 hours and baste with the liquid mixture once every 30 minutes.

7. Once it is done, remove the smoked Portobello mushrooms from the smoker and place on a serving dish.

8. Baste the smoked Portobello mushrooms with the remaining liquid then serve.

9. Enjoy!

SMOKED TOMATO WARM SOUP

(TOTAL COOK TIME 1 HOUR 15 MINUTES)

INGREDIENTS FOR 10 SERVINGS

- Red Tomatoes (2-lbs., 0.907-kgs)

The Spice

- Olive oil – 1 tablespoon
- Chopped onion – 1 cup
- Vegetable broth – 3 ½ cups
- Tomato puree – ¾ cup
- Thyme – 1 teaspoon
- Minced garlic – 1 tablespoon
- Bay leaf – 1
- Salt – ¼ teaspoon
- Black pepper – ½ teaspoon

The Heat

- Mesquite wood

METHOD

1. Prepare the smoker for indirect heat and set the temperature to 225°F (107°C).

2. Cut the tomatoes on top and once the smoke is ready, place the tomatoes on the rack inside the smoker with the cut sides down.

3. Close the smoker and smoke the red tomatoes for 30 minutes.

4. Once it is done, remove the smoked tomatoes from the smoker and let it cool.

5. Preheat a saucepan over medium heat then pour olive oil into the saucepan.

6. Once the oil is hot, stir in chopped onion and minced garlic then sauté until lightly golden brown and aromatic.

7. Pour vegetable broth into the saucepan then add smoked tomato, tomato puree, thyme, bay leaf, salt, and black pepper. Bring to boil.

8. Once it is boiled, remove from heat and let it cool for approximately 15 minutes.

9. Using an immersion blender blend the soup until smooth then strain through a sieve.

10. Return the smooth soup to the saucepan then bring to a simmer.

11. Transfer to a serving bowl then serve.

12. Enjoy warm!

Smoked Cauliflower Oregano

(total cook time 2 Hours 5 Minutes)

Ingredients for 10 servings

- Cauliflower (2.5-lbs., 1.133-kgs)

The Spice

- Olive oil – 3 tablespoons

- Salt – ½ teaspoon

- Pepper – ½ teaspoon

- Oregano – 1 ½ tablespoons
- Dried basil – ¾ tablespoon

THE HEAT

- Apple wood

METHOD

1. Prepare the smoker for indirect heat and set the temperature to 200°F (93°C). Wait until the smoke is ready.

2. In the meantime, cut the cauliflower into small pieces and remove the core.

3. Place the cauliflower in a disposable aluminum pan then drizzle olive oil over the cauliflower. Toss until the cauliflower florets are completely coated with olive oil.

4. Sprinkle salt, pepper, oregano, and basil on top then place the aluminum pan in the smoker.

5. Smoke the seasoned cauliflower florets for 2 hours and stir occasionally.

6. Once it is done, remove the smoked cauliflower florets from the smoker and transfer to a serving dish.

7. Serve and enjoy warm.

Salty and Juicy Smoked Jalapeno

(TOTAL COOK TIME 2 HOURS 5 MINUTES)

INGREDIENTS FOR 10 SERVINGS

- Jalapeno (2-lbs., 0.907-kgs)

THE GLAZE

- Olive oil – 3 tablespoons

THE SPICE

- Salt – 1 ½ teaspoons

THE DIP

- Apple Cider Vinegar

THE HEAT

- Apple wood

METHOD

1. Prepare the smoker for indirect heat and set the temperature to 200°F (93°C).

2. Coat the jalapenos with olive oil then arrange on the rack inside the smoker while the smoker is still cold.

3. Smoke the jalapenos for 2 until 3 hours depending on your desired. Once the smoked jalapenos are done, the last temperature will be around 200°F (93°C).

4. Remove the smoked jalapenos from the smoker and dip in the apple cider vinegar.

5. Take the smoked jalapenos out of the apple cider then arrange on a serving dish.

6. Sprinkle salt on top then serve.

Lemon Garlic Smoked Artichoke

(total cook time 1 Hour 15 Minutes)

Ingredients for 10 servings

- Artichokes (2.5-lbs., 1.133-kgs)

The Glaze

- Olive oil – 1 ¼ cups

- Lemon juice – ½ cup

- Minced garlic – 3 tablespoons

- Salt – ¼ teaspoon

- Pepper – ¼ teaspoon

THE HEAT

- Mesquite wood

METHOD

1. Remove the outer leaves of the artichokes then cut the ¼ of the artichokes.

2. Next, remove the artichoke's steam then cut then into halves lengthwise.

3. Preheat your steamer over medium heat then arrange the halved artichokes in the steamer.

4. Steam the halved artichokes for approximately 20 minutes or until tender.

5. Once it is done, remove the steamed artichokes from the steamer then let them cool to room temperature.

6. Prepare the smoker for indirect heat and set the temperature to 200°F (93°C). Wait until the smoke is ready.

7. In the meantime, pour olive oil and lemon juice in a bowl the season with minced garlic, pepper, and salt. Stir until combined.

8. Arrange the artichokes in a disposable aluminum pan then brush each artichoke with the glaze mixture.

9. Smoke the artichokes for an hour then remove from the smoker.

10. Arrange the smoked artichokes on a serving dish then serve.

11. Enjoy!

Smoked Broccoli Crispy

(TOTAL COOK TIME 50 MINUTES)

INGREDIENTS FOR 10 SERVINGS

- Broccoli (2.5-lbs., 1.133-kgs)

THE SPICES

- Olive oil – 6 tablespoons

- Salt – 1 teaspoon

- Pepper – ¾ teaspoon

THE HEAT

- Alder wood

METHOD

1. Prepare the smoker for indirect heat and set the temperature to 375°F (191°C).

2. While waiting for the smoke, cut and trim the broccoli florets and stems then place in a disposable aluminum pan.

3. Drizzle olive oil over the broccoli florets then sprinkle salt and pepper on top.

4. Once the smoke is ready, place the aluminum pan in the smoker and smoke the broccoli for approximately 45 minutes or until the broccoli is tender but still crispy.

5. Once the broccoli is done and smells smoky, remove from the smoker then transfer to a serving dish.

6. Serve and enjoy warm.

CRUNCHY SMOKED ASPARAGUS PAPRIKA

(TOTAL COOK TIME 1 HOUR 35 MINUTES)

INGREDIENTS FOR 10 SERVINGS

- Asparagus (3-lbs., 1.361-kgs)

THE RUB

- Olive oil – 3 tablespoons

- Salt – 1 teaspoon

- Pepper – ¾ teaspoons

- Paprika – 1 ½ tablespoons

THE HEAT

- Apple wood

METHOD

1. Prepare the smoker for indirect heat and wait until it reaches 225°F (107°C).

2. In the meantime, cut and trim the asparagus then rub with olive oil.

3. Sprinkle salt, pepper and paprika over the asparagus then shake until the asparagus is completely coated with spices.

4. Once the smoke is ready, place the asparagus on the rack inside the smoker.

5. Smoke the asparagus for approximately an hour and a half or until the asparagus is tender but still crunchy. Occasionally flip during the smoking time.

6. Once the asparagus is done, remove from the smoker and transfer to a serving dish.

7. Serve and enjoy.

Smoked Cabbage Pumpkin Jalapeno

(TOTAL COOK TIME 1 HOUR 35 MINUTES)

INGREDIENTS FOR 10 SERVINGS

- Cabbage (3.5-lbs., 1.587-kgs)

THE FILLING

- Pumpkin puree – ½ cup
- Minced jalapeno – 2 tablespoons

The Rub

- Paprika – 2 tablespoons
- Coconut sugar – 1 tablespoon
- Chili powder – 1 teaspoon
- Salt – ½ teaspoon
- Black pepper – ¾ teaspoon
- Garlic powder – 1 teaspoon
- Onion powder – 1 teaspoon
- Cumin – ½ teaspoon

The Heat

- Apple wood

METHOD

1. Combine pumpkin puree with minced jalapeno then mix until incorporated.

2. Remove the core of the cabbage then fill it with pumpkin mixture.

3. Next, combine paprika with coconut sugar, chili powder, salt, black pepper, garlic powder, onion powder, and cumin then rub the spice mixture over the outside of the cabbage.

4. Let the cabbage rest for an hour to ensure that the cabbage is completely seasoned.

5. Prepare the smoker for indirect heat and set the temperature to 225°F (107°C).

6. Once the smoke is ready, place the cabbage in the smoker and smoke for an hour and a half.

7. Once the smoked cabbage is done, remove it from the smoker and let it cool for a few minutes.

8. Cut the smoked cabbage into wedges then serve.

9. Enjoy!

MINTY GARLIC SMOKED EGGPLANT DIP

(TOTAL COOK TIME 1 HOUR 10 MINUTES)

INGREDIENTS FOR 10 SERVINGS

- Eggplants (2.5-lbs., 1.133-kgs)

THE SPICES

- Minced garlic – 2 ½ teaspoons

- Chopped mint leaves – ½ cup

- Coconut yogurt – ¾ cup

- Olive oil – 3 tablespoons

THE HEAT

- Mesquite wood

METHOD

1. Cut the eggplants into halves lengthwise then set aside.

2. Prepare the smoker for indirect heat and set the temperature to 225°F (107°C).

3. Once the smoke is ready, place the eggplants on the rack inside the smoker with the cut sides down.

4. Smoke the eggplant for approximately 45 minutes to an hour or until the eggplants are tender.

5. Remove the smoked eggplants from the smoker and let them cool for a few minutes.

6. Scoop out the smoked eggplant flesh then mash until smooth.

7. Add minced garlic and chopped mint leaves to the mashed eggplant then drizzle coconut yogurt and olive oil on top. Stir until combined.

8. Serve and enjoy with smoked vegetables.

SPINACH AND WALNUTS SMOKED STUFFED MUSHROOMS

(TOTAL COOK TIME 1 HOURS 10 MINUTES)

INGREDIENTS FOR 10 SERVINGS

- Portobello mushroom (2.5-lbs., 1.133-kgs)

THE FILLING

- Toasted walnuts – ½ cup
- Chopped basil – 1 cup

- Chopped spinach – 2 cups

- Chopped garlic – 1 tablespoon

- Lemon juice – 11 ½ tablespoons

- Salt – ¼ teaspoon

THE HEAT

- Apple wood

METHOD

1. Place toasted walnuts in a food processor then process until smooth.

2. Add chopped basil, chopped spinach, garlic, lemon juice, and salt then process again until combined.

3. Spoon the walnuts and spinach mixture into the mushroom's cavities then arrange in a disposable aluminum pan. You may need more filling, depends on the size of the mushrooms.

4. Prepare the smoker for indirect heat and set the temperature to 250°F (121°C).

5. Once the smoker is ready, place the disposable aluminum pan in the smoker.

6. Smoke the mushrooms for an hour until the mushrooms are tender. It depends on the size of the mushrooms.

7. Once it is done, remove the smoked stuffed mushrooms from the smoker and transfer to a serving dish.

8. Serve and enjoy.

SMOKED TOMATO SAUCE CHIPOTLE

(TOTAL COOK TIME 1 HOUR 15 MINUTES)

INGREDIENTS FOR 10 SERVINGS

- Red Tomatoes (2-lbs., 0.907-kgs)

THE SPICE

- Garlic cloves – ¼ cup

- Chipotle– ½ teaspoon

- Olive oil – 2 tablespoons

- Balsamic vinegar – ¼ teaspoon

- Salt – ¼ teaspoon

- Black pepper – ¼ teaspoon

THE HEAT

- Alder wood

METHOD

1. Prepare the smoker for indirect heat and set the temperature to 225°F (107°C).

2. Core the tomatoes and fill each tomato with garlic clove then place in a disposable aluminum pan.

3. Once the smoke is ready, place the disposable aluminum pan in the smoker and smoke the tomatoes for approximately an hour or until the tomatoes are soft and the skin are darkened. The tomatoes will also release their juice.

4. Remove the smoked tomatoes from the smoker and let it cool.

5. Transfer the smoked tomatoes together with garlic and juices then add chipotle, olive oil, and balsamic vinegar.

6. Season the mixture with salt and pepper then blend until smooth.

7. The tomato sauce is ready to use.

8. Enjoy with smoked vegetables or pasta.

Marinated Spicy Smoked Whole Cauliflower

(TOTAL COOK TIME 4 HOURS 5 MINUTES)

INGREDIENTS FOR 10 SERVINGS

- Cauliflower (3.5-lbs., 1.587-kgs)

THE RUB

- Olive oil – ¼ cup

- Smoked paprika – 1 tablespoon

- Lemon juice – 3 tablespoons

- Cumin – ½ tablespoon

- Cayenne pepper – 1 ½ tablespoons

- Minced garlic – 3 tablespoons

- Tomato puree – 3 tablespoons

THE HEAT

- Apple wood

METHOD

1. Place smoked paprika, lemon juice, cumin, cayenne pepper, minced garlic, and tomato puree in a bowl then mix well.

2. Pour olive oil over the mixture and stir until becoming a paste.

3. Remove the cauliflower leaves then rub the spice paste all over the cauliflower.

4. Marinate the cauliflower for 2 hours and store in the fridge to keep it fresh.

5. After 2 hours, prepare the smoker for indirect heat and set the temperature to 200°F (93°C).

6. Take the cauliflower out of the fridge then thaw at room temperature.

7. Once the smoke is ready, place the seasoned cauliflower in the smoker and smoke for 2 hours.

8. Once finished, remove the smoked cauliflower from the smoker and let it sit for a few minutes.

9. Cut the smoked cauliflower into thick slices like cakes then arrange on a serving dish.

10. Serve and enjoy.

SMOKED ASPARAGUS WITH CREAMY GARLIC

(TOTAL COOK TIME 1 HOUR 40 MINUTES)

INGREDIENTS FOR 10 SERVINGS

- Asparagus (3-lbs., 1.361-kgs)
- Sliced onion – 1 ½ cups

THE SAUCE

- Coconut oil – ¼ cup
- Minced garlic – 2 ½ tablespoons
- Lemon juice – ¼ cup

- Salt – ¼ teaspoon
- Black pepper – ½ teaspoon

THE HEAT

- Maple wood

METHOD

1. Cut and trim the asparagus then set aside.

2. Prepare the smoker for indirect heat and wait until it reaches 250°F (121°C).

3. Meanwhile, preheat a saucepan over medium heat then add coconut oil to the saucepan.

4. Once the coconut oil is melted, stir in minced garlic then sauté until aromatic and lightly golden brown.

5. Remove the saucepan from heat and let the sautéed garlic cool.

6. Season sautéed garlic with salt and black pepper then drizzle lemon juice over it. Mix well.

7. Spread sliced onions in a disposable aluminum pan then spread the asparagus over the sliced onions.

8. Drizzle garlic sauce on top then place the disposable aluminum pan in the smoker.

9. Smoke the asparagus for about an hour and a half or until tender.

10. Once it is done, remove the smoked asparagus from the smoker then transfer to a serving dish.

11. Drizzle the liquid sauce on top then serve.

12. Enjoy!

SMOKED BELL PEPPER WITH GINGERY TOFU AND QUINOA

(TOTAL COOK TIME 1 HOUR 15 MINUTES)

INGREDIENTS FOR 10 SERVINGS

- Bell pepper (3-lbs., 1.361-kgs)

THE FILLING

- Cooked quinoa – 2 cups

- Diced tofu – 1 cup

- Grated carrots – 2 tablespoons

- Chopped cilantro – ¼ cup

- Soy sauce – 3 tablespoons

- Chopped scallions – 2 tablespoons

- Minced garlic – 2 teaspoons

- Ginger – 2 teaspoons

- Coconut sugar – 1 teaspoon

- Sesame oil – 1 ½ tablespoons

THE HEAT

- Mesquite wood

METHOD

1. Preheat a pan over medium heat then pour sesame oil into the pan.

2. Once the oil is hot, stir in minced garlic then sauté until lightly golden brown and aromatic.

3. Remove the pan from heat then add cooked quinoa, chopped cilantro, grated carrots, chopped scallions, and tofu to the pan.

4. Season with soy sauce, ginger, and coconut sugar then mix well.

5. Prepare the smoker for indirect heat and set the temperature to 300°F (149°C).

6. Cut the bell peppers into halves lengthwise then fill each halved bell pepper with the quinoa and tofu mixture.

7. Once the smoke is ready, arrange the stuffed bell peppers directly on the rack inside the smoker and smoke for an hour.

8. When it is done, take the smoked stuffed bell peppers out of the smoker then arrange on a serving dish.

9. Serve and enjoy!

Smoked Cabbage BBQ

(total cook time 2 Hours 15 Minutes)

Ingredients for 10 servings

- Cabbage (4-lbs., 1.814-kgs)

The Filling

- Diced onions – ½ cup

- Balsamic vinegar – 3 tablespoons

- Salt – ¼ teaspoon

- Black pepper – ½ teaspoon
- Coconut oil – ¼ cup

THE GLAZE

- Organic ketchup – 2 tablespoons
- Apple cider vinegar – ¾ tablespoon
- Lemon juice – 1 teaspoon
- Coconut sugar – 1 teaspoon
- Worcestershire sauce – 1 teaspoon
- Mustard – 1 teaspoon
- Pepper – ¼ teaspoon
- Smoked paprika – ¼ teaspoon
- Onion powder – ¼ teaspoon
- Garlic powder – ¼ teaspoon
- Chili powder – ¼ teaspoon
- Water – 1 ½ tablespoons

THE HEAT

- Apple wood

Method

1. Place the entire glaze ingredients—organic ketchup, apple cider vinegar, lemon juice, coconut sugar, Worcestershire sauce, mustard, pepper, smoked paprika, onion powder, garlic powder, chili powder, and water in a saucepan. Stir until incorporated then bring to a simmer.

2. Remove the glaze from heat and let it cool.

3. Prepare the smoker for indirect heat and set the temperature to 225°F (107°C). Wait until the smoke is ready.

4. In the meantime, combine coconut oil with balsamic vinegar, salt, and black pepper then mix well.

5. Remove the core of the cabbage then fill the hole with diced onion.

6. Drizzle coconut oil mixture over the onions then glaze the cabbage with the glaze mixture.

7. Wrap the cabbage with aluminum foil but let it open on the top.

8. Place the wrapped cabbage in the smoker and smoke for an hour and a half. Keep the temperature stable.

9. After an hour and a half, completely wrap the cabbage around the head then smoke for about 30 minutes more.

10. Once it is done, remove the smoked cabbage from the smoker and let it cool for a few minutes.

11. Unwrap the smoked cabbage and cut into wedges.

12. Serve and enjoy.

CHAPTER 2 - FRUIT

SWEET SMOKED AVOCADO WITH TEA AROMA

(TOTAL COOK TIME 15 MINUTES)

Ingredients for 10 servings

- Ripe avocados (3.5-lbs., 1.587-kgs)

The Water Bath

- Coconut sugar – ¾ cup
- Oolong tea – 2 cups

The Heat

- Maple wood

Method

1. Prepare the smoker for indirect heat and set the temperature to 250°F (121°C).

2. Pour oolong tea into a water pan then add coconut sugar to the pan. Stir until dissolved.

3. Once the smoke is ready, place the pan with tea mixture on the lowest rack in the smoker and wait until the smoke generates tea aroma.

4. Cut the ripe avocados into halves then remove the seeds.

5. Arrange the halved avocados on the rack inside the smoker with the cut sides down.

6. Smoke the halved avocados for 10-15 minutes according to the size of the avocados then remove from the smoker.

7. Arrange the smoked avocados on a serving dish then serve.

8. Enjoy!

CINNAMON SMOKED APPLE DESSERT

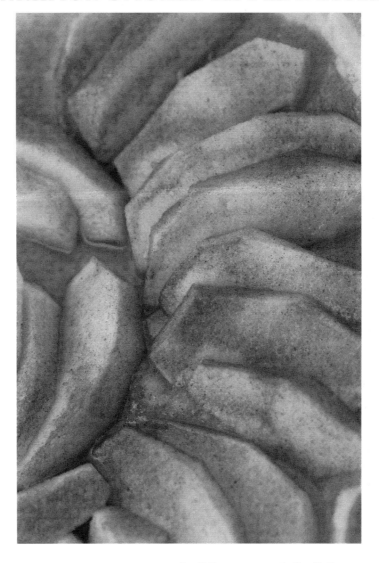

(TOTAL COOK TIME 1 HOUR 40 MINUTES)

INGREDIENTS FOR 10 SERVINGS

- Red Apples (2.5-lbs., 1.133-kgs)

THE GLAZE

- Olive oil – 3 tablespoons
- Maple syrup – ¼ cup
- Coconut sugar – 3 tablespoons
- Ginger – ½ teaspoon
- Cinnamon – 2 teaspoons

THE HEAT

- Apple wood

METHOD

1. Combine olive oil with maple syrup then add coconut sugar, ginger, and cinnamon. Stir well then set aside.

2. Prepare the smoker for indirect heat then set the temperature to 300°F (149°C).

3. Core the red apples then cut into thick slices.

4. Once the smoker is ready, arrange the sliced apples on the rack inside the smoker then baste with the glaze mixture.

5. Smoke the sliced apples for an hour and a half or until the apples are soft. Flip and baste the apple with the glaze mixture once every7 20 minutes.

6. Once it is done, remove the smoked apples from the smoker and arrange on a serving dish.

7. Serve as dessert.

SMOKED PINEAPPLE WITH COCONUT CARAMEL SAUCE

(TOTAL COOK TIME 15 MINUTES)

INGREDIENTS FOR 10 SERVINGS

- Ripe pineapples (3.5-lbs., 1.587-kgs)

THE GLAZE

- Olive oil – 3 tablespoons

The Sauce

- Coconut Sugar – ¼ cup
- Water – ¼ cup

The Heat

- Apple wood

Method

1. Place coconut sugar in a saucepan then preheat over very low heat.

2. Once the coconut sugar is melted, pour water into the saucepan then stir until dissolved. Remove from heat and let it cool.

3. Prepare the smoker for indirect heat then set the temperature to 400°F (204°C). Wait until the smoke is ready.

4. In the meantime, peel the pineapples then cut into wedges. Wash and clean the pineapples then pat them dry.

5. Brush the pineapples with olive oil and once the smoke is ready, arrange the pineapples on the rack inside the smoker.

6. Smoke the pineapples for 3 minutes then flip them.

7. Continue smoking the pineapples until the pineapples are browned and smoky. It usually will take around 10 minutes.

8. Once it is done, remove the smoked pineapples from the smoker and quickly baste with coconut caramel.

9. Serve and enjoy.

LEMON CRUMBLES SMOKED PEAR

(TOTAL COOK TIME 50 MINUTES)

INGREDIENTS FOR 10 SERVINGS

- Pear (3-lbs., 1.361-kgs)

THE GLAZE

- Lemon juice – 3 tablespoons

THE FILLING

- Vegan graham cracker crumbs – ½ cup

- Coconut sugar – ¼ cup

- Olive oil – 3 tablespoons

- Grated lemon zest – 1 teaspoon

- Cinnamon – ½ teaspoon

- Nutmeg – ½ teaspoon

THE HEAT

- Maple wood

METHOD

1. Cut the pears into halves lengthwise then remove the seeds.

2. Brush the cut sides of the halved pear with lemon juice to avoid browning then set aside.

3. Place Vegan graham crackers crumbs in a food processor then add coconut sugar, olive oil, grated lemon zest, cinnamon, and nutmeg. Process until combined.

4. Fill the pear cavities with the breadcrumbs mixture then set aside.

5. Preheat the smoker for indirect heat and set the temperature to 300°F (149°C).

6. Once the smoke is ready, place the stuffed pears on the rack inside the smoker then smoke for approximately 45 minutes to an hour.

7. Once the smoked pears are done, remove them from the smoker and arrange on a serving dish.

8. Serve and enjoy.

SMOKED APPLE PUREE WITH NUTMEG AND PEPPER

(TOTAL COOK TIME 1 HOUR 10 MINUTES)

INGREDIENTS FOR 10 SERVINGS

- Apples (4-lbs., 1.814-kgs)

THE SPICES

- Nutmeg – 1 teaspoon
- Pepper – ½ teaspoon

- Coconut sugar – 2 tablespoons

- Maple syrup – 3 tablespoons

- Lemon juice – 3 tablespoons

- Olive oil – 2 tablespoons

The Heat

- Apple wood

Method

1. Prepare the smoker for indirect heat then set the temperature to 300°F (149°C). Wait until the smoke is ready.

2. Cut the apples into quarters and remove the seeds.

3. Once the smoke is ready, place the quartered apples on the rack inside the smoker and smoke for an hour or until the apples are tender.

4. Remove the smoked apples from the smoker then cut into small pieces.

5. Place the smoked apple cubes in a food processor then pour maple syrup, lemon juice, and olive oil over the apples.

6. Season with nutmeg, pepper, and coconut sugar then process until smooth.

7. Serve and enjoy.

CHAPTER 3 - CARBS

SMOKED YELLOW SWEET POTATOES

(TOTAL COOK TIME 1 HOUR)

INGREDIENTS FOR 10 SERVINGS

- Yellow Sweet Potatoes (4-lbs., 1.814-kgs)

THE GLAZE

- Coconut oil – ¾ cup

- Maple syrup – 6 tablespoons

- Salt – 1 teaspoon

THE HEAT

- Maple wood

METHOD

1. Prepare the smoker for indirect heat then set the temperature to 200°F (93°C). Wait until the smoke is ready.

2. Combine coconut oil with maple syrup then season with salt. Stir until incorporated.

3. Cut the sweet potatoes into halves lengthwise then baste each part with the glaze mixture.

4. Wrap each sweet potato with heavy-duty aluminum foil then prick at several places.

5. Once the smoke is ready, arrange the wrapped sweet potatoes on the rack inside the smoker and smoke for about 50 minutes to an hour or until tender.

6. When the smoked sweet potatoes are done, remove from the smoker and let it cool for approximately 10 minutes.

7. Carefully unwrap the smoked sweet potatoes then arrange on a serving dish.

8. Serve and enjoy.

SWEET AND SALTY SMOKED CORN

(TOTAL COOK TIME 1 HOUR 5 MINUTES)

INGREDIENTS FOR 10 SERVINGS

- Corn with the husk (6-lbs., 2.722-kgs)

THE GLAZE

- Olive oil – ¾ cup

- Onion powder – 3 tablespoons

- Sweet paprika – 1 ½ tablespoons

- Coconut sugar – 3 tablespoons

- Chili powder – 1 ½ tablespoons

- Salt – ½ tablespoon

THE HEAT

- Alder wood

METHOD

1. Add onion powder, sweet paprika, coconut sugar, chili powder, and salt to a cup of olive oil then stir until combined.

2. Prepare the smoker for indirect heat then set the temperature to 225°F (107°C). Wait until the smoke is ready.

3. Pull back the husk from each corn and once the smoke is ready, place the corn on the rack inside the smoker.

4. Smoke the corn for approximately 45 minutes to an hour depending on the size of the corn. Baste with the spiced olive oil once every 15 minutes.

5. Once it is done, remove the smoked corn from the smoker and quickly baste with the remaining olive oil mixture.

6. Arrange on a serving dish then serve.

7. Enjoy!

SMOKED POTATOES BBQ HERB

(TOTAL COOK TIME 1 HOUR 5 MINUTES)

INGREDIENTS FOR 10 SERVINGS

- Potatoes (5-lbs., 2.268-kgs)

THE RUB

- Sage – ¼ cup

- Minced garlic – ¼ cup

- Chopped parsley – ¼ cup

- Salt – 3 tablespoons

- Black pepper – 2 tablespoons

- Coconut sugar – 3 tablespoons

- Paprika – 3 tablespoons

THE HEAT

- Hickory wood

METHOD

1. Prepare the smoker for indirect heat and set the temperature to 250°F (121°C). Wait until the smoke is ready.

2. Meanwhile, wash and rinse the potatoes then pat them dry.

3. Cut the potatoes into medium cubes then set aside.

4. Combine sage with minced garlic, chopped parsley, salt, black pepper, coconut sugar, and paprika then mix well.

5. Rub the potato cubes with the spice mixture and make sure that the potatoes are completely coated with the spice mixture.

6. Wrap the potatoes with heavy-duty aluminum foil and prick the aluminum foil at several places.

7. Once the smoke is ready, place the wrapped potatoes in the smoker and smoke for approximately an hour to an hour and a half. The smoked potatoes should be tender.

8. Remove the smoked potatoes from the smoker and let it rest for about 10 minutes.

9. Carefully unwrap the smoked potatoes and transfer to a serving dish.

10. Serve and enjoy.

CHAPTER 4 - NUTS

SMOKED ALMONDS WITH SALT

(TOTAL COOK TIME 35 MINUTES)

INGREDIENTS FOR 10 SERVINGS

- Whole almonds (5-lbs., 2.268-kgs)

THE RUB

- Olive oil – ½ cup

- Liquid smoke – 3 tablespoons

- Multi-purpose flour – 6 tablespoons
- Salt – 6 tablespoons

THE HEAT

- Mesquite wood

METHOD

1. Prepare the smoker for indirect heat and set the temperature to 225°F (107°C). Wait until the smoke is ready.

2. Place the whole almonds in a bowl then drizzle olive oil over the almonds.

3. Sprinkle liquid smoke, flour, and salt over the almonds then toss to combine.

4. Once the smoker is ready, transfer the seasoned almonds to a basket then place the basket on the rack inside the smoker.

5. Smoke the almonds for 30 minutes. Don't forget to stir and flip the almonds once every 10 minutes.

6. When the smoked almonds are done, remove from the smoker then transfer to a serving dish.

7. Serve and enjoy!

SMOKED MAPLE AND GINGER PECANS

(TOTAL COOK TIME 3 HOURS 10 MINUTES)

INGREDIENTS FOR 10 SERVINGS

- Pecans (5-lbs., 2.268-kgs)

THE RUB

- Olive oil – ½ cup

- Maple syrup – ½ cup

- Ginger – 2 tablespoons

- Salt – 1 teaspoon

THE HEAT

- Mesquite wood

METHOD

1. Prepare the smoker for indirect heat and set the temperature to 225°F (107°C). Wait until the smoke is ready.

2. Combine olive oil with maple syrup then season with ginger and salt. Stir until incorporated.

3. Drizzle the maple syrup mixture over the pecans then toss to combine. Make sure that the pecans are completely coated with maple syrup mixture.

4. Place the seasoned pecans in a basket then smoke the pecans for 30 minutes. Flip and stir the pecans once every 10 minutes.

5. Once it is done, remove from the smoker and let the smoked pecans rest for 2 hours.

6. Serve and enjoy.

SPICY CINNAMON SMOKED CASHEWS

(TOTAL COOK TIME 40 MINUTES)

INGREDIENTS FOR 10 SERVINGS

- Cashews (5-lbs., 2.268-kgs)

THE RUB

- Chili powder – 3 teaspoons

- Cinnamon – 3 tablespoons

- Coconut sugar – ½ cup

- Olive oil – ½ cup

- Maple syrup – ¾ cup

- Salt – 1 tablespoon

THE HEAT

- Mesquite wood

METHOD

1. Prepare the smoker for indirect heat and set the temperature to 225°F (107°C). Wait until the smoke is ready.

2. Place the cashews in a basket then smoke for 20 minutes.

3. In the meantime, combine olive oil with maple syrup then season with salt, coconut sugar, cinnamon, and chili powder. Mix well.

4. After 20 minutes, remove the basket with smoked cashews from the smoker then transfer the cashews to a disposable aluminum pan.

5. Drizzle the maple syrup mixture over the smoked cashews then toss to combine.

6. Return the aluminum pan with cashews to the smoker and smoke for another 15 minutes.

7. Once it is done, remove the smoked cashews from the smoker then transfer to a serving dish.

8. Serve and enjoy.

CHAPTER 5 - OTHERS
SMOKED WHEAT MEAT BARBECUE

(TOTAL COOK TIME 3 HOURS 10 MINUTES)

INGREDIENTS FOR 10 SERVINGS

- Vital wheat gluten – 3 cups
- Nutritional yeast flakes – ½ cup
- Cold water – 2 ¼ cups
- Low sodium soy sauce – ½ cup
- Ketchup – 2 tablespoons
- Minced garlic – 2 teaspoons
- Grated lemon zest – 2 teaspoons
- Paprika – 1 tablespoon
- Cumin – ½ teaspoon
- Black pepper – 2 teaspoons
- Chili powder – 1 teaspoon

THE LIQUID

- Cold water – 10 cups
- Low sodium soy sauce – ¼ cup

THE RUB

- Paprika – ¼ cup
- Black pepper – 2 tablespoons

- Chili powder – 2 tablespoons

- Garlic powder – 1 tablespoon

- Onion powder – 1 tablespoon

- Cayenne pepper – ½ tablespoon

- Dry mustard – ½ tablespoon

THE SAUCE

- Water – 1 ½ cups

- Cider vinegar – 1 ½ cups

- Ketchup – ¾ cup

- Red pepper flakes – ½ tablespoon

- Black pepper – 1 teaspoon

- Salt – ½ teaspoon

THE HEAT

- Hickory wood

METHOD

1. Place vital wheat gluten with nutritional yeast then mix well. Set aside.

2. In another bowl, combine low sodium soy sauce, ketchup, minced garlic, grated lemon zest, paprika, cumin, black pepper, and chili powder then pour water over the ingredients. Stir until incorporated.

3. Pour the liquid mixture over the dry mixture then mix until combined and becoming dough.

4. Knead the dough for a few minutes until elastic then let it rest for 10 minutes.

5. Shape the dough into a log then cut into thick slices. Set aside.

6. Pour 10 cups of cold water into a pot then combine with soy sauce.

7. Slowly put the sliced dough in the pot and make sure that it is completely submerged. Bring to boil.

8. Once it is boiled, reduce the heat and bring to a simmer for approximately an hour. Remove from heat.

9. Let it cool for about 15 minutes then take the wheat meat out of the pot.

10. Once the wheat meat is cool, squeeze one by one to discard the excessive liquid.

11. Wrap each wheat meat with plastic wrap then refrigerate for at least 6 hours.

12. To start smoking, set the smoker for indirect heat and wait until the smoke is ready. Set the temperature to 225°F (107°C).

13. Meanwhile, combine the rub ingredients—paprika, black pepper, chili powder, garlic powder, onion powder, cayenne pepper, and chili powder then mix well.

14. Coat the wheat meat with the spice mixture then place on the rack inside the smoker.

15. Smoke the wheat meat for an hour and a half. Occasionally rotate the wheat meat to develop a beautiful golden brown color.

16. In the meantime, combine the barbecue sauce ingredients in a bowl then stir until incorporated.

17. Once the smoked wheat meat is done, remove it from the smoker then place on a serving dish.

18. Let it cool for about 5 minutes then drizzle the sauce on top.

19. Serve and enjoy!

SWEET SMOKED FIRM TOFU

(TOTAL COOK TIME 1 HOUR 10 MINUTES)

INGREDIENTS FOR 10 SERVINGS

- Firm tofu (3-lbs., 1.361-kgs)

THE MARINATE

- Soy sauce – 6 tablespoons

- Maple syrup – ½ cup

- Sesame oil – 2 teaspoons

- Olive oil – 6 tablespoons

- Mustard – 2 tablespoons

- Water – 6 tablespoons

THE HEAT

- Maple wood

METHOD

1. Combine soy sauce with maple syrup, sesame oil, olive oil, mustard, and water then stir until incorporated.

2. Cut the tofu into thick slices then marinate the tofu in the spice mixture. Let the tofu rest for approximately 30 minutes.

3. Prepare the smoker for indirect heat and set the temperature to 225°F (107°C).

4. Once the smoke is ready, place the tofu on the rack inside the smoker.

5. Smoke the tofu for 20 minutes then flip them.

6. Smoke the tofu for another 20 minutes until both sides of the tofu are lightly golden brown.

7. Once it is done, remove the smoked tofu from the smoker then arrange on a serving dish.

8. Serve and enjoy.

CHAPTER 5 - VEGAN LIFESTYLE

Vegan has become a recent trend to lead a healthy and fit life. But what is so special about this diet?

Usually, a vegan diet is abbreviated to a vegetarian diet but that is not the right definition. A vegan diet is a purely plant-based diet and thus, it doesn't contain any food that comes from animals and this also includes eggs and dairy products. So, foods and beverages containing only vegetables, fruits, nuts, grains, and millets is the part of the well-balanced vegan diet. A few decades ago, veganism was only limited to diet but now, due to its amazing health benefits, individuals are opting for it as a lifestyle. Along with food, they are being more focused on using plant-based medication, personal care items, makeup, and clothes. But cutting off meat would means no protein in the diet. Not at all, say hello to your new protein source that is known as legumes. Furthermore, they are vegan products like tofu and tempeh that are similar to meat in texture and taste.

Since famous celebrities have transformed their lives going vegan, is that reason enough to turn to veganism? Along with this reason, there are scientific evidence to prove life-changing benefits a vegan lifestyle bring. Obviously reducing carbon footprint and being kind to an animal are in fact major benefits, but veganism is so much more. Following are some of the important effects of having clean eating based on plants:

- Treating obesity by shedding weight
- Improving hypertension (blood pressure)
- Lowering cholesterol in the blood
- Reducing the risk of coronary disease
- Control diabetes
- Improves digestion
- Sleep gets better
- Clear and glowing skin
- Higher energy levels

This is the good stuff that comes from choosing a vegan lifestyle but the path is not rosy if you are not careful. In the beginning, you can feel weakness, fatigue, intense craving, hunger pangs, headache and stomach aches. Don't worry these symptoms go away if you are eating enough calories and once your body gets used to the meat-free diet. But if they don't seem to go away, see a doctor immediately.

A vegan diet is worth giving a shot by those individuals who are feeling sluggish or concern about their cholesterol or blood sugar level. You can even simply try it to know what a plant-based diet can do for you. The transition to a vegan lifestyle is gradual and needs all the patience. Just keep your goals in mind and always remember why you are choosing veganism.

WHAT TO EAT AND AVOID?

You can eat

1- all types of vegetables,
2- All types of fruits
3- Grains as in bread, rice, pasta, barley, couscous, and Ferro.
4- All types of legumes
5- All types of nuts and seeds and using them for butter.
6- Tofu and tempeh in place of meat.
7- Plant-based oil like olive oil, sesame oil.
8- The sweetness of maple syrup, agave syrup, and coconut sugar.

What can you not eat?

1- Animals are completely off limits along with seafood.
2- For eggs, try tofu.
3- Replace dairy cheese with cheese obtained from nuts like cashew cheese.
4- A great milk substitute is almond milk or coconut milk.
5- Don't use honey for sweetener.
6- For fats or oils, avoid using fish oil or lards.
7- Processed foods.

FOOD ITEMS EVERY VEGAN SHOULD LOOK OUT FOR

When buying vegan staples for the kitchen, look out for:

- Bread that comes with **egg wash** finishing.
- Dough prepared with **egg yolks** or protein from **dairy**.
- Sauces - Worcestershire sauce with **anchovies**.
- Salad dressing – any **dairy** products using in preparing ranch dressing.
- Condiments – **cheese** in pesto.
- **White sugar** in ingredients or juices.
- Deep fried food using **egg** batter or **animal fat** for frying.
- Sweets containing gelatins.
- Alcohols made with fish gelatin

That's a big list and you may take vegan as an expensive diet. It will become heavy for your wallet if you pile your food cart with processed items, ready-made or frozen foods, vegan cheeses or mock meats but it won't be if you are consuming real food. Real food means food made at home with fresh vegetables, legumes, and grains. A vegan diet containing real food is generally based on

- Variety of vegetables and fruits every day, at least in five portions.
- More than 50% carbohydrates as in meals based on bread, pasta or potato.
- Proteins from beans and pulses.
- Add whole grains where possible
- Low-sugar soy drinks or low-fat yogurt
- A small amount of unsaturated oil and spreads
- 6-8 cups of water every day

CHAPTER 6 - BARBECUE

Barbecue, in short BBQ, is a cooking apparatus and presentation of a food style for cooking and serving. Mostly, it is meat which is cooked by using a cooking machine called barbecue grill. The cooking method involves smoking meat in the outdoor and the source of heat can be wood, charcoal, a mixture of these two, gas or electricity. In comparison to baking which is done with moderate cooking temperature in an oven, barbecue takes long cooking time and is done at low temperature.

Barbecue is such a versatile cooking method that it is practiced throughout the world. Every region has its own version of barbecue and food specialty but they have the same cooking concept of smoking food outside and over the fire. It has become a part of the tradition, especially for America where it is held during small informal gatherings or formal events.

TECHNIQUES OF BARBECUE

There are four distinct types of cooking technique for barbecue.

1- Smoking: Originally, barbecue involves cooking food using smoke at a low temperature between the ranges of 240 to 280 degrees F. This cooking technique is smoking. The food needs several hours until reached to the desired internal temperature. This cooking technique not only adds flavor to smoke but also preserve it by exposing food to smoke from wood. Most of the smoked food is meat and seafood, along with vegetables, fruits, and nuts.

2- Grilling: Barbecue-grill is cooking food over direct heat, either from above or below. The cooking temperature is over 500 degrees F and lasts for a few minutes. Thus, this technique is effective to cook food quickly. The heating source is charcoal, wood, gas or electricity. It is quite similar to smoking with the only difference in cooking temperature. Smoking is done at low temperature whereas grilling needs high temperature.

3- Roasting: Barbecue-roasting technique uses a baking oven or convection heat to cook meats. This means surrounding food with hot air to cook. The cooking temperature is moderate and last for 1 to 2 hours. It is used to cook meats, casserole, and bread.

4- Braising: Barbecue-Braising technique involves cooking food at a different speed. This means, food first starts cooking quickly, then it slows down, it speeds up again. The cooking time last for a few hours. Meats and vegetables are added to a pot which is then placed on top of the grill. The heat is given by gas or electricity. The major advantage of barbecue brazing is soft meat, falling from the bone, as meat is cooked three times.

CHAPTER 7 - VEGAN BARBECUE

Like mentioned above, barbecue is mostly comprised of meat dishes and this is a bad news for vegans. Good news! Vegans don't have to give up the barbecue for cutting out meat from their lives.

A vegan can still enjoy a hot and delicious barbecue food without disturbing their diet. Barbecuing food isn't all always burgers, vegetables are made for grilling! And knowing that no animal is the harm in this process makes it much more scrumptious.

INTERESTING TIPS AND TRICKS FOR A SUCCESSFUL MEAT-FREE BARBECUE

Barbecue without meat is a little different and is all about creativity. So make sure that your vegan barbecue goes great with these quick tips.

1- Not all vegan food is suited for cooking. Therefore, do read cooking instructions on the food package and see if it is meant for a barbecue or not.

2- Prepare barbecue grill first because you will not like your food sticking to the grilling rack. This is also the secret for tastiest barbecue. Clean grilling rack and scrape off any bits or pieces on it. Then brush or spray grilling rack with oil generously before adding food in it.

3- For greasing grilling rack or food, grape seed oil is a great choice.

4- Always go for a no-hassle vegan barbecue. Use natural flavored food for this like Portobello mushrooms, asparagus, and corn on the cob, marinated tofu, pineapple rings or vegetable foil packets.

5- Give every vegetable a shot of barbecue instead of sticking to usual like corn, eggplant, and tomatoes. Try vegetables that are different in taste because once they started caramelized and crispy, you will be surprised how tasty they turn out.

6- A great meat alternate for vegans is tofu. To grill it, make sure it is drained, well pressed and extra-firmed. Furthermore, grease grill rack with oil laboriously or else it will get stuck on it.

7- Add barbecue tools to your kitchen set. Tongs are basting brush are the keys for a great barbecue. Also, purchase some disposable aluminum foil pans or grill basket for barbecuing small vegetables like green beans and olives. Just let them heat up properly before adding your food in it.

8- Keep your barbecue simple and cheap. Don't spend too much on the ingredients and pick fresh ingredients that can whip up a quick and delicious barbecue meal. All you need is to brush vegetables with grapeseed oil, seasoned generously with salt and black pepper. Fancy things up by using fresh herbs or spice mix and let them grill.

And, you will feel full and great!

CHAPTER 8 - INFORMATION ABOUT SMOKING FOOD

WHAT IS THE PRIMARY DIFFERENCE BETWEEN BARBECUING A MEAT AND SMOKING IT?

You might not believe it, but there are still people who think that the process of Barbecuing and Smoking are the same! So, this is something which you should know about before diving in deeper.

So, whenever you are going to use a traditional BBQ grill, you always put your meat directly on top of the heat source for a brief amount of time which eventually cooks up the meal. Smoking, on the other hand, will require you to combine the heat from your grill as well as the smoke to infuse a delicious smoky texture and flavor to your meat. Smoking usually takes much longer than traditional barbecuing. In most cases, it takes a minimum of 2 hours and a temperature of 100 -120 degrees for the smoke to be properly infused into the meat. Keep in mind that the time and temperature will obviously depend on the type of meat that you are using, and that is why it is suggested that you keep a meat thermometer handy to ensure that your meat is doing fine. Keep in mind that this method of barbecuing is also known as "Low and slow" smoking as well. With that cleared up, you should be aware that there are actually two different ways through which smoking is done.

THE CORE DIFFERENCE BETWEEN COLD AND HOT SMOKING

Depending on the type of grill that you are using, you might be able to get the option to go for a Hot Smoking Method or a Cold Smoking One. The primary fact about these three different cooking techniques which you should keep in mind are as follows:

- **Hot Smoking:** In this technique, the food will use both the heat on your grill and the smoke to prepare your food. This method is most suitable for items such as chicken, lamb, brisket etc.
- **Cold Smoking:** In this method, you are going to smoke your meat at a very low temperature such as 30 degree Celsius, making sure that it doesn't come into the direct contact with the heat. This is mostly used as a means to preserve meat and extend their life on the shelf.
- **Roasting Smoke:** This is also known as Smoke Baking. This process is essentially a combined form of both roasting and baking and can be performed in any type of smoker with a capacity of reaching temperatures above 82 degree Celsius.

THE DIFFERENT TYPES OF AVAILABLE SMOKERS

Essentially, what you should know is that right now in the market, you are going to get three different types of Smokers.

Charcoal Smoker

These types of smokers are hands down the best one for infusing the perfect Smoky flavor to your meat. But be warned, though, that these smokers are a little bit difficult to master as the method of regulating temperature is a little bit difficult when compared to normal Gas or Electric smokers.

Electric Smoker

After the charcoal smoker, next comes perhaps the simpler option, Electric Smokers. These are easy to use and plug and play type. All you need to do is just plug in, set the temperature and go about your daily life. The smoker will do the rest. However, keep in mind that the finishing smoky flavor won't be as intense as the Charcoal one.

Gas Smokers

Finally, comes the Gas Smokers. These have a fairly easy mechanism for temperature control and are powered usually by LP Gas. The drawback of these Smokers is that you are going to have to keep checking up on your Smoker every now and then to ensure that it has not run out of Gas.

THE DIFFERENT STYLES OF SMOKERS

The different styles of Smokers are essentially divided into the following.

Vertical (Bullet Style Using Charcoal)

These are usually low-cost solutions and are perfect for first-time smokers.

Vertical (Cabinet Style)

These Smokers come with a square shaped design with cabinets and drawers/trays for easy accessibility. These cookers also come with a water tray and a designated wood chips box as well.

Offset

These type of smokers have dedicated fireboxes that are attached to the side of the main grill. The smoke and heat required for these are generated from the firebox itself which is then passed through the main chamber and out through a nicely placed chimney.

Kamado Joe

And finally, we have the Kamado Joe which is ceramic smokers are largely regarded as being the "Jack Of All Trades".

These smokers can be used as low and slow smokers, grills, hi or low-temperature ovens and so on.

They have a very thick ceramic wall which allows it to hold heat better than any other type of smoker out there, requiring only a little amount of charcoal.

These are easy to use with better insulation and are more efficient when it comes to fuel control.

THE DIFFERENT TYPES OF CHARCOAL

In General, there are essentially three different types of Charcoals. All of them are basically porous residues of black color that are made of carbon and ashes. However, the following are a little bit distinguishable due to their specific features.

- **BBQ Briquettes:** These are the ones that are made from a fine blend of charcoal and char.
- **Charcoal Briquettes:** These are created by compressing charcoal and are made from sawdust or wood products.
- **Lump Charcoal:** These are made directly from hardwood and are the most premium quality charcoals available. They are completely natural and are free from any form of the additive.

THE CORE ELEMENTS OF SMOKING!

Smoking is a very indirect method of cooking that relies on a number of different factors to give you the most perfectly cooked meal that you are looking for. Each of these components is very important to the whole process as they all work together to create the meal of your dreams.

- **Time**: Unlike grilling or even Barbequing, smoking takes a really long time and requires a whole lot of patience. It takes time for the smoky flavor to slowly get infused into the food. Jus to bring things into comparison, it takes an about 8 minutes to fully cook a steak through direct heating, while smoking (indirect heating) will take around 35-40 minutes.

- **Temperature:** When it comes to smoking, the temperature is affected by a lot of different factors that are not only limited to the wind, cold air temperatures but also the cooking wood's dryness. Some smokers work best with large fires that are controlled by the draw of a chimney and restricted airflow through the various vents of the cooking chamber and firebox. While other smokers tend to require smaller fire with fewer coals as well as a completely different combination of the vent and draw controls. However, most smokers are designed to work at temperatures as low as 180 degrees Fahrenheit to as high as 300 degrees Fahrenheit. But the recommend temperature usually falls between 250 degrees Fahrenheit and 275 degrees Fahrenheit.

- **Airflow:** The level of air to which the fire is exposed to greatly determines how your fire will burn and how quickly it will burn the fuel. For instance, if you restrict air flow into the firebox by closing up the available vents, then the fire will burn at a low temperature and vice versa. Typically in smokers, after lighting up the fire, the vents are opened to allow for maximum air flow and is then adjusted throughout the cooking process to make sure that optimum flame is achieved.

- **Insulation:** Insulation is also very important when it comes to smokers as it helps to easily manage the cooking process throughout the whole cooking session. A good insulation allows smokers to efficiently reach the desired temperature instead of waiting for hours upon hours!

CONCLUSION

I can't express how honored I am to think that you found my book interesting and informative enough to read it all through to the end. I thank you again for purchasing this book and I hope that you had as much fun reading it as I had writing it. I bid you farewell and encourage you to move forward and find your true Smoked Food spirit!

GET YOUR FREE GIFT

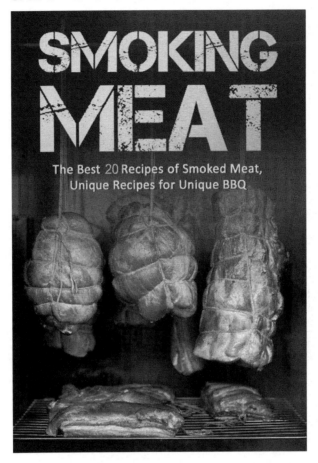

Suscribe to our Mail List and get your FREE copy of the book

'Smoking Meat: The Best 20 Recipes of Smoked Meat, Unique Recipes for Unique BBQ'

http://tiny.cc/smoke20

OTHER BOOKS BY ADAM JONES

https://www.amazon.com/dp/1720321590

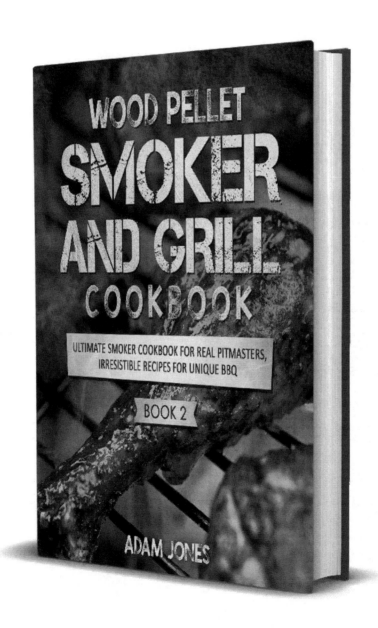

HTTPS://WWW.AMAZON.COM/DP/1725577690

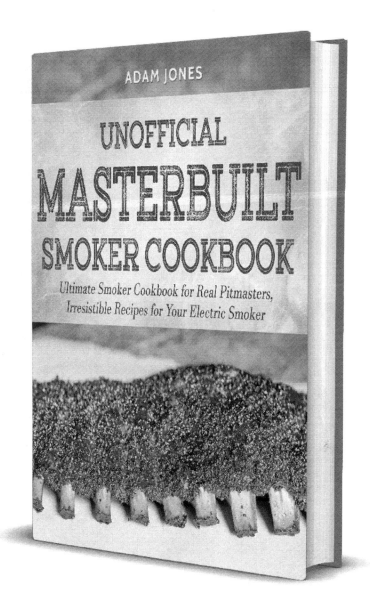

HTTPS://WWW.AMAZON.COM/DP/1723009849

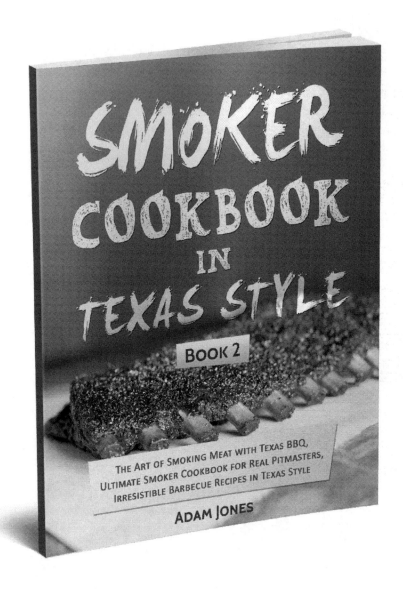

HTTPS://WWW.AMAZON.COM/DP/B07DJ8XZT9

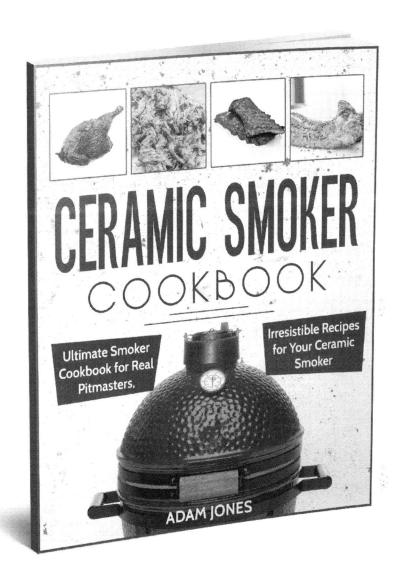

HTTPS://WWW.AMAZON.COM/DP/B07DJ62MZP

https://www.amazon.com/dp/198756605X

https://www.amazon.com/dp/1548040959

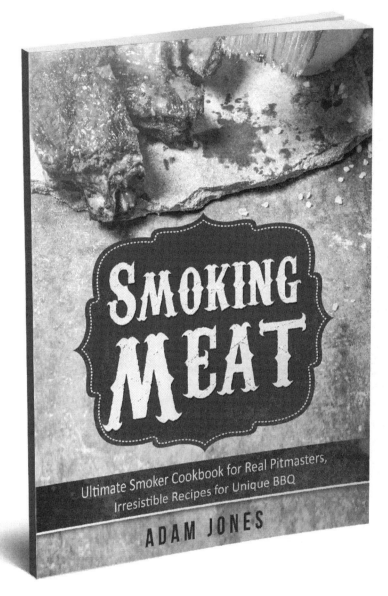

https://www.amazon.com/dp/B07B3R82P4

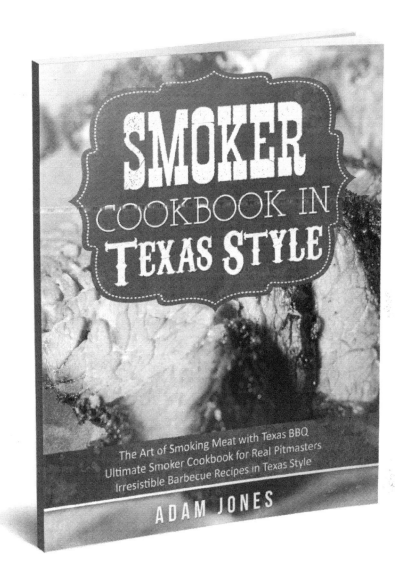

https://www.amazon.com/dp/B07B4YDKJ5

https://www.amazon.com/dp/1979559902

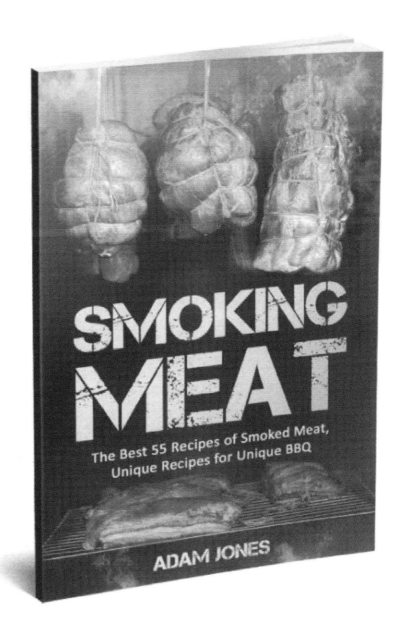

https://www.amazon.com/dp/1544791178

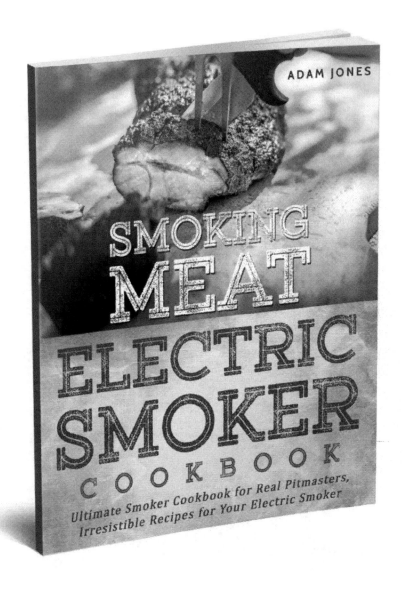

https://www.amazon.com/dp/1979811318

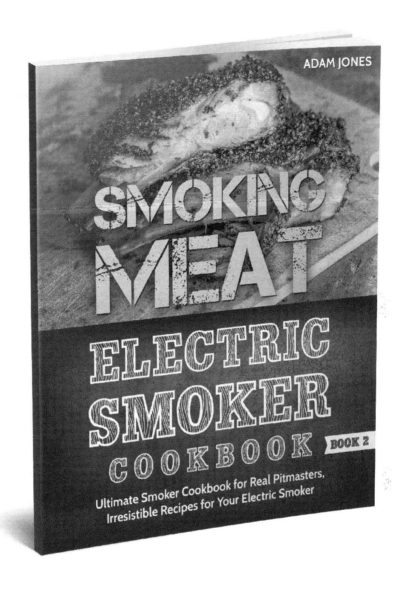

https://www.amazon.com/dp/1981617973

https://www.amazon.com/dp/1546605916

https://www.amazon.com/dp/1981940693

https://www.amazon.com/dp/1977677347

https://www.amazon.com/dp/1542597846

https://www.amazon.com/dp/154418199X

P.S. Thank you for reading this book. If you've enjoyed this book, please don't shy, drop me a line, leave a feedback or both on Amazon. I love reading reviews and your opinion is extremely important for me.

My Amazon page: www.amazon.com/author/adjones

ISBN: 9781719934817

Disclaimer and Terms of Use:*The effort has been made to ensure that the information in this book is accurate and complete, however, the author and the publisher do not warrant the accuracy of the information, text, and graphics contained within the book due to the rapidly changing nature of science, research, known and unknown facts and the internet. The Author and the publisher do not hold any responsibility for errors, omissions or contrary interpretation of the subject matter herein. This book is presented solely for motivational and informational purposes only.*

Made in the USA
Lexington, KY
19 December 2018